Carole & Jim
TO

Something to talk
about after 40 years!
FROM
XO
Linda & Frank

Editorial Director: Todd Hafer
Editor: Megan Langford
Art Director: Kevin Swanson
Designer: Myra Colbert Advertising & Design: Myra Colbert, Kevin Marozas
Illustrator: Maria O'Keefe
Production Artist: Dan Horton

ISBN: 978-1-59530-203-8

BOK2097

Printed and bound in the United States of America

An amusing
and informative collection
of facts, trivia, and things
that'll make you say

"I
never knew
THAT!"

DAVID HOFFMAN

GIFT BOOKS
from Hallmark

Military toilet paper is printed

with a camouflage pattern

because standard-issue white

could attract enemy fire

at a very vulnerable time. ❶

Kleenex was originally manufactured

as filters for gas masks during World War I.

In the aftermath, Kimberly-Clark promoted them

as both coffee filters and cold cream removers

until research showed that most people

had taken to using them like handkerchiefs

to blow their noses. ❶

The standard blue

United States Postal Service mailbox

holds approximately

four thousand letters. ●

Bubble Wrap was the result

of a failed attempt in 1957

by two engineers

to invent a washable,

textured plastic wallpaper. ❗

When Richard Reynolds

started manufacturing

his eponymous aluminum foil,

it wasn't to package and store food.

He made it for his uncle,

cigarette magnate R. J. Reynolds,

who was in need of a way

to wrap tobacco

and keep it fresh. ❶

Assigned to cover the 1933 Indianapolis 500,

a Denver journalist called his Colorado newspaper

and promised, "... will overhead winner,"

meaning he would send the name of the winner

via the overhead wires (the telegraph).

The editor, however, misunderstood the message

and interpreted it to mean

that the name of the winner was 'Will Overhead.'

As a result, the headline running in the *World Independent*

the next morning read,

"Overhead Wins Indianapolis Race." ❶

The only Major League Baseball teams

with names that don't end

with the letter "s"

are the Boston Red Sox

and the Chicago White Sox. ⚠

According to numerous

pediatric dermatologists,

duct tape is an effective,

non-painful method

for removing warts. !

Although synonymous with French gastronomy,

the baguette was actually invented in Vienna.

It only arrived in Paris in the 1850s

when steam-injection ovens —

essential for getting the crust right —

finally came to France. ●

Alexander Graham Bell

never set out to invent the telephone.

It was a by-product of his efforts

to create a device

that might help his wife and mother,

both of whom were deaf,

hear and communicate better. ❶

The inspiration for Post-it Notes

came to a 3M scientist not while on the job,

but while singing in the church choir —

after the pieces of paper

he used to mark his place in his hymnal

repeatedly fell out. ❗

The Ford Model T wasn't black

because of the paint colors

available at the time,

but because black paint

was both cheaper and dried faster

than other colored paints. ●

In the film *Back to the Future*,

the time-travel device that sent Marty McFly

from 1985 to 1955 (and back again)

was originally written to be a refrigerator,

not a DeLorean.

The portal was changed to a car

for fear that kids might emulate the film

and start playing in refrigerators. ❗

Fonzie's motorcycle in *Happy Days*

was the same one

Steve McQueen rode

in *The Great Escape.* ❶

The U.S. cereal industry

uses more than 800 million

pounds of sugar per year.

That's more than

three pounds per person! ❶

The creator of Eudora,

the first e-mail software program,

was Steve Dorner, a staff member

at the University of Illinois at Urbana-Champaign.

The University not only gave the software away,

but Dorner, who was salaried,

received no stock options

and no royalties on his 1988 creation. ⚠

It is the aromatic leaves of the violet —

not the petals —

that are used to make perfume. ❶

A muskmelon that was brought

from Armenia to Italy in the fifteenth century

was planted and cultivated

in the gardens of a papal estate near Rome.

The estate was Cantaluppi,

so the fruit crop that resulted

became known as cantaloupe. ●

There are more than

7,500 varieties of apples;

the type that is said

to have struck Sir Isaac Newton

(and consequently inspired

the theory of gravity)

is a large green

Flower of Kent. ❶

Strawberries contain

more vitamin C

than oranges. ❗

Aa is a type of volcanic ash —

and a good word to know

when playing Scrabble. ❶

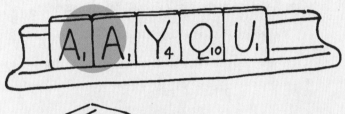

In the early 1800s, it was customary

for local U.S. banks to issue their own money.

Given the large French-speaking population in Louisiana,

the ten-dollar bills that came from that area

frequently had DIX (which is French for "ten")

printed on them.

People began to refer to those bills as "dixies"

and to Louisiana as "Dixie Land."

In time, Dixie became a nickname

applied to all of the Deep South. ❶

Charles Dow, the financial reporter

who founded *The Wall Street Journal*

and created the Dow Jones Industrial Average,

never graduated from high school. ❶

There's a reason it is known
as "passing gas":
the average fart is made up of
59% nitrogen, 21% hydrogen,
9% carbon dioxide, 7% methane,
and 4% oxygen. ⓘ

Only red neon lights

actually contain neon gas.

The yellow lights

contain a sodium gas,

and the blue lights

contain mercury. ❶

Prepackaged salad greens

stay fresh for weeks

on store shelves

because manufacturers

inflate the bags

with nitrogen. ●

It takes

approximately ninety minutes

to hard-boil

an ostrich egg. ❶

The average elephant

produces about fifty pounds

of dung a day. ❗

Everyone knows that a standardized

set of letters is called an alphabet.

They might not know, however,

that the word comes from

the first two letters of the Greek alphabet,

alpha and *beta.* ❶

The first ten moves

of chess

can be played roughly

170,000,000,000,000,000,000,000,000

possible ways. ⓘ

When bookkeepers and brothers

Henry and Richard Bloch decided to start

a company that specialized in tax preparation in 1955,

they feared that customers would

mispronounce their last name as "blotch,"

so they smartly changed the "h" to a "k,"

added their first initials,

and began doing business

as H&R Block. ●

The abbreviation for pound is "lb"

because in ancient Rome

weight was measured in libras;

in Latin records, the libra

was written as "lb." ❶

The fork was invented in Italy

as a utensil

with which to eat pasta.

However, it was unilaterally dismissed

by the Church,

which frowned upon using anything

not created by God

to touch God's bounty. !

The Batmobile was built

on the chassis

of a Chevy Impala. ❗

The "classic" Irish combo of corned beef and cabbage

is more a product of the island of Manhattan

than of the Emerald Isle.

In the early twentieth century,

Irish immigrants to the U.S. settled

on New York's lower east side,

and since the area was predominantly Jewish,

it was difficult to find bacon or cured ham

to go with their cabbage.

So they did what their neighbors did —

bought brisket, brined it in kosher salt,

and served "corned beef" for dinner. ❶

The three dots in the Domino's Pizza logo

represent the company's first three locations.

The original concept was that a dot

would be added for each new store that opened —

a plan that ran out of steam

as the design ran out of space. ●

More pizzas are sold and delivered

on Super Bowl Sunday

than on any other day of the year —

a primary reason that Super Bowl Sunday

ranks second (behind Thanksgiving)

as the biggest day for food consumption

in the United States. ❶

To say something is

"as American as apple pie"

doesn't really make a lot of sense

when you consider

that apple pie originated

in France and England. ●

David Letterman funds a scholarship

at his alma mater,

Ball State University in Muncie, Indiana,

that provides financial assistance

to "C" students, based solely

on their creativity

rather than their grades. ❗

Époisses de Bourgogne,

an unpasteurized cow's-milk cheese

whose rind is soaked in brandy,

is so pungent that it has been banned

from the Paris Metro. ⓘ

Vieux Boulogne,

a soft cheese from Northern France,

is — according to a panel

of nineteen human taste testers

and one "electronic nose"

(a machine equipped with sensors

to detect different chemical aromas) —

the smelliest cheese

in the world. ❗

The famous two-toned French manicure

isn't really French at all.

Hollywood makeup artist Jeff Pink

got the idea from Parisian runway models,

who simply rubbed a white pencil

beneath their unpolished fingernail tips

to give them a clean,

natural look. !

The "funny bone"

didn't get its name

because it makes us laugh,

but because its real name

is the humerus. ❗

When President Harry Truman —

a Democrat —

visited Disneyland in 1957,

he refused to ride on Dumbo,

as he did not wish to be photographed

with a giant elephant,

the symbol of the Republican Party. ❶

Dwight D. Eisenhower

wore red pajamas

that had the

five gold stars of a general

embroidered on the collar.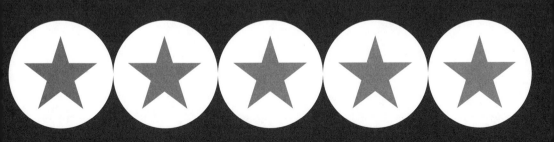

David Rice Atchison

was the President of the United States

for one day, March 4, 1849.

James Polk's term ended that morning,

but President-elect Zachary Taylor

refused to be sworn in on a Sunday.

In the interim, the job automatically

went to Atchison,

the Senate president pro tem. ❶

Former Secretary of State

Colin Powell

grew up in a predominantly

Jewish neighborhood in the Bronx

and, as a result,

is highly proficient

in speaking Yiddish. ❶

American dentists

use 26,000 pounds of gold

per year for fillings,

crowns, and inlays.

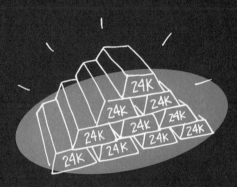

Both President Lyndon Johnson

and tenor Luciano Pavarotti

spent several years

as elementary school teachers

after graduating from college. ❗

When the $1.5 billion

Hubble Space Telescope's antenna

was damaged during launching,

NASA scientists on Earth

relied on a model built

from Tinkertoys and a lamp cord

to figure out how to fix it. ●

One of the first models

for the artificial heart

was invented in the early 1950s

at the Yale University School of Medicine,

using the parts and motor

from a standard Erector Set. ❶

While searching for a way

to store hydrogen and other gases

needed for his chemistry experiments,

London professor Michael Faraday

invented the balloon in 1824. ❶

According to mathematicians,

a standard deck of cards

needs to be shuffled seven times

to adequately randomize

the cards. ❶

The first folding game board was devised

by a chess-loving priest in the twelfth century.

At the time, the Church viewed chess as gambling

and threatened to excommunicate

any member of the clergy caught playing,

so the priest cleverly created

a special board that closed

to resemble two books

lying on top of each other. ❶

Illinois Avenue

has been mathematically proven

to be the square

on the Monopoly game board

that has the highest probability

of being occupied by a player.

The "Go" square

comes in second. ●

Parcheesi can be traced back

to sixteenth-century India,

when bored factory workers

realized that a piece of cloth

with a unique pattern

could be turned into a game

that would help pass time. ❶

Honey never spoils.

Ever. ❶

In 1945, Harold Mattson and Elliot Handler

combined forces — and their names —

to form Mattel Toys.

Fourteen years later, Handler's wife Ruth

also became an integral part of the operation

when she created a fashion doll

(and the doll's boyfriend),

which she named after their two kids,

Barbie and Ken. ❶

Hawaiians once used kites

to claim pieces of land.

The kites were released in the air,

and ownership was taken

wherever the kite fell. ❗

Created in England in the 1760s,

the first jigsaw puzzles were maps.

Pieces were formed by cutting

along the borders of the countries,

and the end result was used

to teach kids geography. ❗

When French explorer Jacques Cartier

asked some native Iroquois where they lived,

they replied "kanata," meaning "village."

However, Cartier mistakenly thought

they were telling him the name of the entire region,

which is how the territory he claimed

along the St. Lawrence River in 1536

(and the subsequent colony he set up)

came to be known as Canada. ❶

Charles Rushmore was a young attorney

sent from New York City

to South Dakota in 1885 to check

on mining titles in the Black Hills.

When he singled out one of the mountains

and inquired about its name,

his guide, William Challis, shot back

that it did not have one,

but suggested they could

"just call the damn thing Rushmore." ●

Not only was the couple depicted

in the painting *American Gothic*

not husband and wife

(or father and daughter),

they weren't even farmers.

The man was artist Grant Woods's dentist;

the woman was Woods's sister. ⚠

The original selling price

of *Mona Lisa* in 1519

was 4,000 écus,

equivalent to $105,000

by today's economic standards.

The current estimated value

is $670 million. ●

Attendance at the Louvre rose

from an average of 6 million visitors in 2000

to 7.5 million in 2005.

Museum officials are mum on the matter,

but most in the art world call this

"The Da Vinci Code Effect,"

attributing the visitor increase (and interest)

to the novel by Dan Brown

that sold more than 61 million copies

in 44 languages. ⬤

Built in 1903,

the first Harley-Davidson motorcycle

used a tomato can

for a carburetor. ❗

Leonardo DiCaprio was named

after artist Leonardo da Vinci.

Apparently, DiCaprio's pregnant mother

was standing in front of a da Vinci painting

at the Uffizi Gallery in Florence

when DiCaprio first kicked. ❶

In 1866, Claude Monet,

plagued by debt, burned two hundred

of his own paintings to prevent them

from being seized

by creditors. ❶

Before inventing the telegraph,

Samuel Morse was a portrait painter

and a professor

in the art department

at New York University. ⓘ

Prior to earning his master's degree

in experimental animation,

SpongeBob SquarePants creator

Stephen Hillenburg

taught marine biology

at the Orange County Ocean Institute

in Dana Point, California. !

The white-shingled house

that Ari Gold lived in

for the first four seasons of *Entourage* was,

for nearly thirty years,

the real-life residence

of Ozzie and Harriet Nelson. ❶

Except for the red nose and the wild tufts of hair,

Krusty the Clown on *The Simpsons*

is a dead ringer for Homer for good reason:

the original concept behind Krusty

was that he was secretly Homer in disguise;

and while Homer got no respect from his son,

Bart worshiped Krusty,

unaware it was his dad beneath the makeup.

But production was on such a tight schedule

in the early days of the series

that creator Matt Groening found the explanation

too complicated and dropped the concept. ❶

The bottle in which Jeannie lived

on *I Dream of Jeannie*

was fashioned from a

1964 Christmas-edition

Jim Beam decanter. ❗

The Emmy Award derives its name

from the Immy —

a slang term for the image orthicon,

a tube that was used

in television cameras

until the 1960s. ❶

The penny is the only

currently minted U.S. coin

featuring a profile

that faces to the right. ❗

The mask worn

by killer Michael Myers

in the movie *Halloween*

was, in fact, a mask

of William Shatner's face

(as *Star Trek's* Captain James Kirk)

spray-painted white. ⓘ

While filming *Star Trek*, director Joe Pevney

asked Leonard Nimoy to improvise a hand sign

to accompany Spock's Vulcan farewell,

"Live long and prosper."

The gesture he came up with —

right hand lifted, palm facing out,

with the fingers separated into a V shape —

is an obscure Rabbinical blessing Nimoy

remembered from his youth.

Its significance is that it represents the Hebrew letter "shin,"

which is the twenty-first letter of the Hebrew alphabet

and a symbol for the word "Shaddai,"

a name for God. ❗

In the twelfth century,

modern tennis was born when monks

introduced a racquet into the handball game

that they played against monastery walls.

The name came later, however,

when French nobility latched onto the sport

and their servants took to calling *tenez*

(which translates to "hold on" or "take heed")

just before the ball

was tossed into play. ❗

Dr. Benjamin Spock,

the renowned pediatrician

and author,

won a gold medal

in the 1924 Olympics

as a rower. ❶

The first ballet originated

during the Italian Renaissance

of the late fifteenth century,

surfacing as a dance interpretation

of fencing. ❶

Irish step dancing

(now recognizable worldwide, thanks to *Riverdance*)

was created after the British conquest

of Ireland in the 1600s outlawed music

and cultural traditions had to be performed secretly.

The dance form that evolved —

body and arms kept stationary, movement confined to the feet —

ensured that if the English glanced

at the locals through a window,

they would be unable to tell

that anyone was dancing. ①

Albert Einstein's facial characteristics

inspired the look of three

popular film characters:

E.T. had Einstein's eyes,

Yoda had his forehead,

and Emmett Brown in *Back to the Future*

had his hair. ❗

The term "paparazzi"

comes from Federico Fellini's *La Dolce Vita*.

In the film, Marcello Mastroianni

writes a gossip column,

and Walter Santesso plays his coworker,

a tabloid photographer

whose name is Paparazzo. ❶

The ruby slippers

that Judy Garland wore

as Dorothy in *The Wizard of Oz*

were Ferragamo pumps. ❗

In 1966, the Scott Paper Company
introduced a paper dress, a special offer
available through the mail for one dollar.
Within six months, they had sold
five hundred thousand of them —
prompting experts to predict that by 1980,
twenty-five percent of all our clothes
would be made of paper. ⓘ

Steve Martin honed his talent for crafting balloon animals,

a staple of his early stand-up act,

while working at Disneyland's Main Street Magic Shop

in the early 1960s.

Also employed by the park at that time was Ron Ziegler,

the future press secretary of Richard Nixon,

who did duty as a skipper

on the Jungle Cruise. ❶

When Mexican vaqueros

described the hats they wore

as *tan galán* (meaning "so elegant"),

the Texas cowboys who had also taken

to wearing them misunderstood —

and their signature headgear

became known as the "ten-gallon" hat.

Despite the name, however,

a ten-gallon hat only holds

about three quarts. ⓘ

Costumed characters commonly found

at amusement parks are known

in the industry as "fuzzies."

On the average, a fuzzie's outfit

weighs forty pounds,

and during the hot summer months,

under the blazing sun

and surrounded by crowds,

interior temperatures can heat up

to 150 degrees. ●

The comb-over,

a method for styling hair to cover bald areas

using only the individual's own hair,

was invented in 1977

by Frank and Donald Smith

of Orlando, Florida.

The Smiths hold a U.S. patent

for the comb-over (No. 4,022,227),

complete with instructional diagrams. ❶

The use of the term "bigwig"

to imply a person of great importance

dates back to eighteenth-century England,

when men of great influence

relied on the size of their wigs

to flaunt their wealth

and social status. ⓘ

Before the 1900s,

people rarely wore wristwatches.

Men carried pocket watches

and women often attached watch fobs to their dresses.

During World War II, however,

the Army issued wristwatches to soldiers

in order to give them quicker access to time,

and when these veterans returned home,

they brought the watches back

and popularized them. ❶

Although often thought

to be a contraction for the phrase

"Swiss watch," the name "Swatch"

actually stems from "second watch"

and the marketing campaign

that introduced it as an inexpensive,

casual, and disposable accessory. ❶

Collarless sweaters that button

down the front were named

for the man who was fond of wearing them —

James Thomas Brudenell, 7th Earl of Cardigan.

In addition to starting a fashion trend,

Brudenell led the famous

Charge of the Light Brigade in 1854,

during the Crimean War. ❶

The military salute evolved

from medieval times,

when knights in armor

would raise their visors

to reveal their identities. ❶

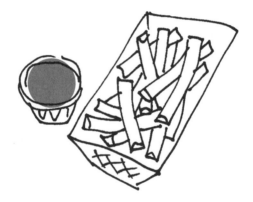

The food most frequently ordered

by women in restaurants is not a salad,

but french fries —

which could explain why,

according to a survey,

most dinner arguments

are caused by one dinner partner

stealing another's fries. ●

Before she found fame

as an author and sex therapist,

Dr. Ruth Westheimer

was trained as a sniper

in the Israeli army. ❗

Although the degree

of effectiveness has been questioned,

a 1985 study at Boston University's

School of Medicine

found that Coca-Cola

worked as a spermicide

and that Diet Coke,

for some reason,

worked even better. ⚠

Many of the coffee bars

    inside the CIA and other top-secret

United States government buildings

    are staffed by blind people,

    although this has as much to do

with a very successful employment drive

    as it does national security. ⚠

Cappuccino is named

for the similarity of its color

to the color of the long, hooded robes

worn by the monks of the Capuchin order —

and the fact that a properly prepared

cappuccino leaves a brown ring

along the rim of the cup

that resembles a monk's cowl. ❶

Chemists have identified

over 250 compounds in wine,

making it more complex

than blood serum. ❶

When soda first hit the market,

the bottles were sealed with a cork.

When the cork was removed,

it made a sound that gave soda

the nickname "pop." ❗

In 1923, Frank Epperson was operating

a lemonade stand at an amusement park

in Oakland, California, when he set out

to market a frozen drink-on-a-stick

concoction he called the Episcle —

a combination of his surname and the word "icicle."

His kids, however, referred to their

dad's novelty treats as "Pop's icles,"

so when Epperson applied for a patent,

he did so under the catchier name, Popsicle. ❶

Louis Pasteur first developed pasteurization

in the 1850s as a way

to prevent wine spoilage.

Only later did he realize

that his method could be used

on other substances, like milk. ❶

Each day,

the flatulence of a single sheep

could power a small truck

for twenty-five miles.

A sheep's digestive process

produces methane gas,

which can be burned as fuel. ❶

It takes an average

of 345 squirts

from a cow's udder

to yield a gallon of milk. ⚠

It is impossible

to "sweat like a pig"

because pigs don't sweat.

This is why pigs can be found

rolling in mud on hot days —

it cools the surface

of their skin. ❗

The man who gave

Jack Russell terriers their name

was Reverend John "Jack" Russell,

an English clergyman

who bred dogs as a hobby.

Although he developed the eponymous

fox terrier offshoot in the 1800s,

the breed wasn't recognized

by the American Kennel Club

until 1997. ❶

Under NBA regulations,

sneakers are the only

article of clothing

a player can wear

that bears a commercial logo. ⚠

The odds

of a good golfer

making a hole in one

are 1 in 8,606,

which averages out to one

in every 478 games. ●

The golf hole

has a standard 4.25" diameter

because that was the size

of the piece of pipe drain

that was used to cut

the first permanent holes

at the Royal and Ancient Golf Club

of St. Andrews in Fife, Scotland. ❶

The speed

of a typical golfer's swing

is 101 miles per hour. ❶

Rain falls

   at a maximum speed

of eighteen miles per hour. ❶

Funeral processions

move at a slow pace

because at one time,

candelabras were carried in the march.

If mourners walked too fast,

the candles would go out.

If you want to make a room

as bright as the sun,

try collecting

14,286,000,000 fireflies. ❗

Fred Astaire's famous dances

with Ginger Rogers were some

of the most romantic moments in movie history,

but Astaire actually developed the numbers

with choreographer Hermes Pan,

who filled in for Rogers during choreography,

then later taught her the steps. ●

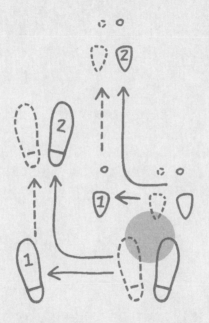

An airplane's "black box"

isn't black.

Rather, it is fluorescent orange

with white stripes,

which makes it

easier to see. ❗

Although it ranks

as the world's fifth-busiest airport,

more people start their trips

at Los Angeles International

than at any other airport

in the world. ❶

The underground interterminal train

that has been operating

at George Bush Intercontinental Airport

in Houston since 1981 replicates

the exact mechanical design

of Disneyworld's Tomorrowland PeopleMover.

It is the only transportation system

outside of a Disney theme park that was built

by the Walt Disney Company. ❶

The airport code for Sioux City, Iowa, is SUX.

Despite the city's ongoing appeal to change it,

so far the Federal Aviation Administration

has refused to do so. ❶

Tomatoes are a member

of the nightshade family,

of which the majority is poisonous.

So, for almost two hundred years

after they were brought back from Mexico,

Europeans were afraid to eat tomatoes.

Instead, they used the plants

as houseplants. ❶

Martial arts actor Bruce Lee

was so fast that many of his scenes

had to be shot in 32 frames per second

(rather than the normal 24 frames per second)

in order to slow down the film

so viewers could see his moves.

Ringo Starr

was a certified cosmetologist

when he replaced Pete Best

as The Beatles's drummer.

He joined the group

hoping to make enough money

to open his own hair salon. ❶

First-class seats were originally found

at the back of the airplane

so that priority passengers

would be as far as possible

from the noise of the piston engines.

After jet service became the norm

in the late 1950s,

noise was no longer an issue,

and first class was moved

to the front. ❗

Prior to making it big as novelists,

Harper Lee (*To Kill a Mockingbird*)

wrote plane tickets as a

reservations agent for Eastern Airlines,

Kurt Vonnegut (*Slaughterhouse Five*)

wrote press releases for General Electric,

and Amy Tan (*The Joy Luck Club*)

wrote horoscopes. ●

The first flight attendants

were men whose main job function

was to handle baggage.

When United Airlines decided

to put women on their planes in 1930,

all of the stewardesses they hired were nurses,

based on the theory that nurses

would be most capable

of handling passengers' needs

on bumpy flights. 🛈

Based on the standard formula,

the Statue of Liberty

would wear a size 879 shoe. ❶

The uniforms worn by The Beatles

on the cover of the album

Sgt. Pepper's Lonely Hearts Club Band

were rental costumes.

The medals that adorn

Paul's and George's jackets, however,

were not only theirs, they were real.

Each of the Fab Four had been awarded

MBE medals (Members of the Order

of the British Empire)

by Queen Elizabeth II in 1965. ❶

The phrase John Lennon

can be heard saying

(twice, on some recordings)

at the end of "Strawberry Fields Forever" —

and the phrase that many Beatles fans

took to be "I buried Paul"

and that helped launch

the "Paul is dead" hysteria —

is actually "cranberry sauce." ❶

The rock song

with more cover versions

than any other

is Paul McCartney's "Yesterday."

It has been recorded

by more than three thousand

different artists. ●

Led Zeppelin's "Stairway to Heaven"

is the most well-known

and popular rock song

to have never been released

as a single. ⊕

In a publicity stunt to recognize

the one million copies sold

of Glenn Miller's *Chattanooga Choo Choo* in 1942,

RCA Records spray-painted a record gold

and presented it to Miller during a radio show.

A decade later, the Recording Industry Association

of America (RIAA) borrowed the idea

and started issuing Gold Records

whenever sales hit five hundred thousand. ●

The first single to officially

be awarded a Gold Record

was Perry Como's "Catch a Falling Star."

The first album to receive the award

was the soundtrack to the film version

of *Oklahoma.* ❶

Musician Gordon Sumner

got the nickname "Sting"

because he once performed

wearing a black-and-yellow rugby shirt

that bandmates said made him

look like a bumblebee. ❗

The Grammy Award-winning

"Killing Me Softly With His Song"

was written about singer-songwriter Don McLean,

although the song referenced in the title

was not his classic "American Pie,"

but the track "Empty Chairs,"

which was released on the flip side

of that single. ❶

The ubiquitous piano ditty "Chopsticks"

was written in 1877

by sixteen-year-old Euphonia Allen.

The name had nothing to do

with Asian eating utensils,

but came from the way she played her composition:

with palms facing inward, the little fingers lowest,

so that the movement

of the hands hitting the keys

mirrored a chopping motion. ●

Leo Fender, designer

of the highly cherished Fender Guitar,

didn't know how to play the guitar. ❶

Joe Sheridan was closing up his restaurant

at Ireland's Foynes Airport in 1945

when bad weather forced a transatlantic flight

to turn around and come back.

Realizing that the plane's passengers

would be tired and irritable, Sheridan stayed late

and greeted them with coffee that had been mixed

with a little sugar, spiked with a shot of Irish whiskey,

and topped with freshly whipped cream.

When asked if what they were drinking was Brazilian coffee,

Sheridan replied, "No. It's Irish coffee."

The name stuck.

Techno-musician

and singer-songwriter Moby

got his pseudonym honestly —

his real name is Richard Melville Hall,

and he's the great-great-grandnephew

of Herman Melville, author of *Moby Dick*.

Hall freely admits he never

got through the book. ❶

When Herman Melville's classic,

Moby Dick, was first published in America,

it bombed, selling only 3,797 copies

in its first thirty-six years in print. ❗

One pound of tea yields

about two hundred servings. ！

It takes approximately

six to eight hundred grapes

to produce one

bottle of wine. ❗

Before Johannes Gutenberg

became famous for publishing

the Bible on his printing press,

he had used the invention

to print playing cards

for gamblers. !

Before becoming known the world over as Dr. Seuss,

Theodor Geisel worked during World War II

as a political cartoonist, and his knack

for social commentary found its way

into many of his children's books.

Adolf Hitler was the inspiration for Yertle the Turtle,

Watergate-era Richard Nixon was the basis

for the tiresome Marvin K. Mooney,

and *Horton Hears a Who* was a parable

for the American postwar occupation of Japan. ❶

Dartmouth student Theodor Geisel

first used the pseudonym "Seuss"

after he was banned from writing

for the university's humor magazine

for violating Prohibition laws.

"Seuss" was both his middle name

and his mother's maiden name.

He later added "Dr." as an acknowledgment

of his father's unfulfilled hopes

that his son would earn

a doctorate at Oxford.

Nine months after reading

a 1954 *LIFE* magazine report

on illiteracy that concluded that children

were not learning to read

because their books were boring,

Dr. Seuss created his classic,

The Cat in the Hat,

using only words culled

from an average first-grader's

vocabulary list. ❶

Mockingbirds traditionally mimic

the sounds and songs of other birds,

but mockingbirds found in New York City

have been known to imitate police sirens,

car alarms, buses,

and the beeping of garbage trucks

being driven in reverse. ❗

The word "nerd"

was coined by Dr. Seuss

in his book,

If I Ran the Zoo. ❗

"Dumbledore," an old English word

for "bumblebee,"

was picked by author J. K. Rowling

as the name of Harry Potter's headmaster

because she imagined him

wandering around the castle,

humming to himself. ⚠

Wicked author Gregory Maguire

chose Elphaba as the name

of the Wicked Witch of the West

in tribute to *Oz* author L. Frank Baum.

The name is a phonetic take

on Baum's initials, L-F-B. ❗

Jerry Siegel and Joe Shuster

were classmates at Glenville High

in Cleveland, Ohio, in 1934

when they came up with

the idea of *Superman*.

Four years later, they signed away

all rights to DC Comics —

for $130. ●

In one early published

version of *Cinderella*,

the wicked stepsister

cuts off her own big toe

in order to fit

into the glass slipper. ❶

"Uncopyrightable" is one of the

two longest words

in the English language

that is composed

of entirely different letters. ❶

The popular Web site Yahoo!

got its name from a word thought up

by Jonathan Swift and used

in his classic, *Gulliver's Travels,*

to mean "rude, unsophisticated, uncouth."

The exclamation point was necessitated by law,

added for trademark purposes

after it was discovered that a brand

of Yahoo barbecue sauce and a line

of Yahoo knives already existed. ❶

Odds are that if you counted

all the letters in this book,

thirteen percent of them

would be Es. ❶

DAVID HOFFMAN is a television writer/producer,

frequent on-camera correspondent, and the author of a dozen books

about popular culture for which, in recent years, he has been paid

to play with toys, challenge untapped cooking skills (with the help

of some big-name chefs), and eat and shop his way across the country.

He lives in Los Angeles, where he likes to pretend

that this is hard work. ●

If you enjoyed this book, let us know 🛈

Please send your comments to:

Hallmark Book Feedback
P.O. Box 419034
Mail Drop 215
Kansas City, MO 64141

Or e-mail us at:

booknotes@hallmark.com